THE YEAR OF THE
FLYING MACHINE,

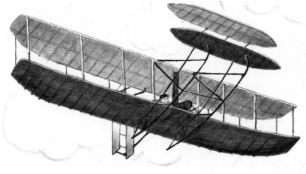

1903,

GENEVIEVE FOSTER,
ILLUSTRATED BY THE AUTHOR

CHARLES SCRIBNER'S SONS
NEW YORK

909.82
F

6.95

Copyright © 1977 Genevieve Foster

Library of Congress Cataloging in Publication Data

Foster, Genevieve Stump, 1893–

The year of the flying machine, 1903.

Includes index.

SUMMARY: Surveys worldwide events and
prominent people during the years 1900 to 1909.

1. History, Modern—20th century—Juvenile
literature.   [1. History, Modern—20th century]

I. Title.

D422.F67   909.82   77-9074

ISBN 0-684-15182-0

CONTENTS

PART 2

PART 3

1900
TO
1909

INTRODUCTION

IN 1900, WHEN THIS CENTURY BEGAN, AIR-planes did not exist. Automobiles were just starting to be manufactured. There was no radio or television. Motion pictures were just beginning to jiggle across the screen. The X ray had been discovered, but radium had not yet been seen. Psychoanalysis had barely been mentioned. And atomic energy was almost inconceivable.

Neither the North nor South Pole had been discovered. The name Lenin had never been heard in Russia, nor had the Russian Communist Party been founded. Kings and emperors ruled all of Europe and Asia, except France and Switzerland. Queen Victoria was head of the powerful British Empire, which extended around the globe.

In the United States, William McKinley was elected President, with Theodore Roosevelt as Vice President. In 1901 McKinley was assassinated; Theodore Roosevelt became President and held the office until 1909.

The first nine years of this century—1900 to 1909—brought amazing changes into our world. This book tells the story of these nine years and of some of the extraordinary people who brought those changes about.

WILBUR · ORVILLE
WRIGHT   ROOSEVELT   MARCONI

MARIE · PIERRE
LENIN   CURIE   FORD

1900 The WRIGHT BROTHERS first went to Kitty Hawk.

1901 MARCONI sent radio waves across the Atlantic.
THEODORE ROOSEVELT became the U.S. President.
LENIN assumed his famous name.

1902 MARIE and PIERRE CURIE isolated radium.

1903 The WRIGHT BROTHERS made their historic flight.
THEODORE ROOSEVELT purchased the Panama Canal.
HENRY FORD and eleven men formed the Ford Motor Company.

1904 Japan started the RUSSO-JAPANESE WAR.

TZU HSI   SUN YAT-SEN   MAO   EINSTEIN

FREUD   JUNG   PEARY   HENSON

1905 ROOSEVELT arranged the Russo-Japanese Peace Treaty.
The RUSSIAN REVOLUTION of 1905 began in January.
CHINA was ruled by the Dowager Empress, Tzu Hsi.
ALBERT EINSTEIN developed his famous equation.

1907 SIGMUND FREUD was visited by CARL GUSTAV JUNG.

1908 ROBERT PEARY started for the North Pole.
The WRIGHT BROTHERS' plane was accepted by the U.S. War
   Dept.
FREUD was honored by an American university.

1909 PEARY and HENSON reached the North Pole.

9

PART I

1900
TO
1902

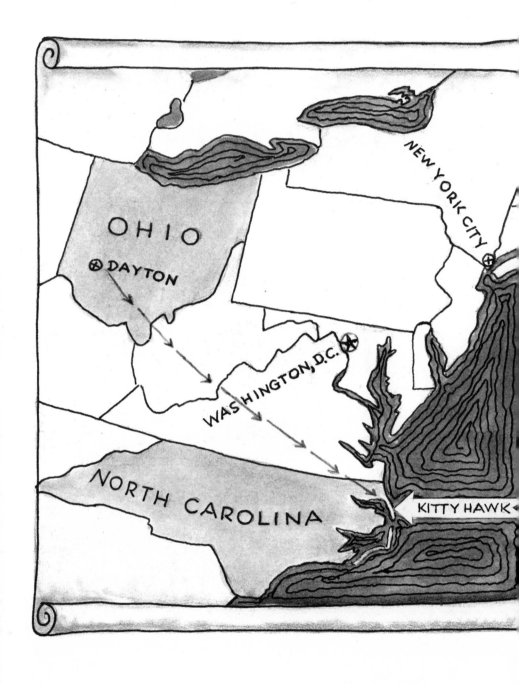

WILBUR ORVILLE

KITTY HAWK IS THE PLACE IN NORTH CARO-
lina where it happened—a great event that was to change
our world. The day was December 17, 1903, bitterly
cold and very windy. There on that windy winter day,
the two Wright brothers, Wilbur and Orville, flew their
power-driven, heavier-than-air machine. In other words,
they flew the world's first airplane! They made four
flights that day—and though the longest one lasted less
than a minute, they knew that they had succeeded. Man's
age-old desire to fly had at last come true!

BISHOP MILTON WRIGHT

THE CHURCH OF
THE UNITED BRETHREN
IN CHRIST

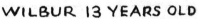

WILBUR 13 YEARS OLD

ORVILLE 9 YEARS OLD

Their father, Bishop Wright, was the first person to hear the good news; they sent a telegram to him at their home in Dayton, Ohio. Their father had given his sons their original interest in flying.

In 1878, when Wilbur was eleven and Orville was seven, he had come home from a short business trip, bringing them a present, which he tossed into the air. Instead of falling to the floor, it rose to the ceiling where it floated for a few minutes before it fell.

It was a toy helicopter, invented by a Frenchman.

Made of cork, bamboo, and paper, it was too fragile to last long, but it was never to be forgotten.

As a boy, Wilbur usually "had his nose in a book," whereas Orville, from the day he skipped kindergarten to tinker with an old sewing machine, was nearly always "up to something," usually hoping to acquire a few extra pennies. First he made kites and sold them to his friends. Then he collected old bones and sold them to a fertilizer company. He gathered metal scraps thrown out by a chain factory and sold them to the junk man.

Once he came upon a collection of stuffed animals in a deserted barn, and decided to put on a circus. Wilbur wrote an ad for the newspaper, giving the exact route of the circus parade, and the price of the tickets. One Christmas, Wilbur gave Orville a set of engraving tools, when he wanted to try making woodcuts. Orville printed a newspaper for his eighth grade. And after high school, he started a printing business and later published a weekly newspaper, of which Wilbur was the editor.

Orville was twenty-one when he came riding home one fine day on a high-wheeled bicycle for which he had paid $160. Six months later, Wilbur found one at auc-

tion for half-price. With this as a start, they decided to buy more, rent a shop, and go into the business of selling bicycles. Soon they began to repair them, and before long they were making their own brand of bicycles, putting them together in the room above the shop.

In 1896, when they had been in the bicycle business four years, they saw the first automobile ever to run on the streets of Dayton. Right away Orville was for building automobiles instead of bicycles.

"Impossible!" said Wilbur. " 'Twould be easier to build a flying machine."

A FLYING MACHINE! To them both flying was an irresistible idea. They had already taken out all the books in the Dayton Public Library about man's attempts to fly. Now they sent to the Smithsonian Institution in

Washington, D.C., for a more complete list of books and articles. They were specially thrilled by the experiments of a German, Otto Lilienthal, who made GLIDERS, in which he went soaring through the air.

In August 1899, the Wright brothers built their first glider, which was like a big biplane kite. Wilbur had noticed that a buzzard kept its balance in the air by twisting its wings. So they built this trick of wing twisting into their glider. Four long cords, attached to the wing tips, were tied to two sticks. The man flying the glider held a stick in each hand, pulling the cords as he saw fit. To test their glider they took it to open fields on the edge of town. After a few trials they saw that they needed a place where there was more wind. They wrote the Weather Bureau in Washington, D.C., and so learned about Kitty Hawk, on the beaches of North Carolina, where a "steady wind" blew in from the sea.

Now they designed a man-carrying glider. The rider was to lie face down on the lower plane, while the other person steadied the glider till it was in the air. Only a few weeks were needed to build it. Cutting and sewing the cloth to cover the wings took the most time.

In the fall of 1900, Wilbur and Orville, full of hope, took their man-carrying glider to Kitty Hawk. To their great disappointment, they found that the wind was not at all "steady." Some days it blew a fearful gale. Most days it was too weak to support a man on the glider. So again the glider had to fly as a kite.

There was no use taking the glider home with them to Dayton, so they left it on the hill and the wife of the village postmaster used the wing covering to make new dresses for her two little girls.

In the summer of 1901, the brothers were back again at Kitty Hawk, with a new glider to ride on. Its wings were larger and more curved. According to everything they had read, it should fly well. But it didn't! Evidently most of the information to be had from books was worthless! Wilbur was about ready to give up.

"Nobody," he said, "will fly for a thousand years."

Besides being discouraged, they had been so plagued by mosquitoes and sand fleas that Orville was more than glad to pack up and go home. However, back in the bicycle shop, they still could not keep from thinking about the glider, wondering why it would not fly.

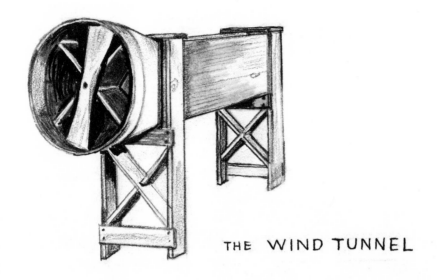

THE WIND TUNNEL

During the winter, the brothers solved the problem by their own experiments. Out of a wooden box and a fan they rigged up a wind tunnel, about sixteen inches square and six feet long. In it they tested miniature planes with wings of various sizes, and set at various angles. From the accurate records they kept, they were able at last to design a glider that would actually fly.

In August 1902, they took their new glider to Kitty Hawk. It flew so well that before they put it away for the winter, they began planning an engine for it. An engine would turn their glider into what they had started out to make—an actual flying MACHINE.

Cartoon from the N.Y. Globe

Theodore Roosevelt

THEODORE ROOSEVELT WAS THE YOUNGEST man ever to become President of the United States, as well as the liveliest, busiest, most dynamic, energetic, and forceful. As President, he considered it not only his right but his duty to do whatever he thought the nation needed unless it was forbidden by the Constitution.

"Speak softly and carry a big stick and you will go far" was an African proverb of which he was very fond. The big stick in his case was the power of the Presidency. Roosevelt swung it first in the direction of "Big Business." For years past, bankers, railroad owners, oil company executives, and mine owners had been growing enormously rich and powerful. There were few laws to control them, so they did as they pleased. Governors, judges, senators deferred to them, because they had the money, or CAPITAL, to finance election campaigns. The working people who did the actual LABOR in the mines and factories were practically disregarded.

In the spring of 1902, 140,000 miners went on strike in the coal mines of Pennsylvania, demanding more pay and better working conditions. In similar strikes, other Presidents had called out the troops and driven the miners back to work.

Theodore Roosevelt called a conference of leaders on both sides, and eventually with the help of J. P. Morgan, the capitalist, they worked out a compromise. Still Roosevelt was not satisfied. He wanted a permanent regulation, so that both labor and management would have a so-called SQUARE DEAL. Therefore he asked Congress to create a Department of Commerce and Labor. Congress refused. So Roosevelt toured the country to tell the people what he was trying to do and why. The people had long felt that it was useless to fight against the combination of big-business executives and crooked politicians. Now they took heart. As a result, after the Congressmen had talked with the folks back home they returned to Washington and passed the bill in a hurry. A new Department of Commerce and Labor was created. The first Secretary of Labor was appointed. The labor leaders were delighted.

One of them who was lunching with the President at the White House remarked:

"At last there is a hearing for us labor fellows."

"Yes," replied the President, "while I am here the White House door will open as easily for the labor man as for the capitalist. And no easier!"

He would not favor one side or the other, so both sides attacked him. Capitalists said he was favoring labor. Labor leaders said he was favoring capital. Wall Street and the Standard Oil Company condemned him as a "radical" out to destroy the Constitution. But radical newspapers, which appealed to the workers, printed stories of how he had secretly "sold out" to the great banker J. P. Morgan.

The President had made bitter enemies among both the very rich and the very poor. But all over the country, people of the great middle class, who were neither too rich nor too poor, stood staunchly behind Theodore Roosevelt, who seemed to be like one of them, as he always claimed to be—just the "average man."

And year by year, he grew more popular. Newspapers were filled with cartoons of him. Photographers snapped him from every angle as he spoke. Strangers from coast to coast spoke of him as "Teddy" or simply "T. R."

Children named their pets for him, and the most popular toy was the "Teddy Bear," which was copied from a bear cub sent to Roosevelt after a hunting expedition in Louisiana.

At the end of his first term, he was hopeful, but not sure, of being re-elected. To his delight he was—and by a far larger majority of votes than any other President had received since Abraham Lincoln!

S S S S   S S S S

IN DECEMBER 1901, THE *NEW YORK TIMES* AN-
nounced "the most wonderful scientific development of
modern times." Marconi, Guglielmo Marconi, the young
Italian inventor, had succeeded in sending signals by
wireless telegraph, now called RADIO, across the Atlantic Ocean. This would be great news for Marconi's
father, who time and again had been disappointed in his
son—this son who had failed to qualify for the Naval

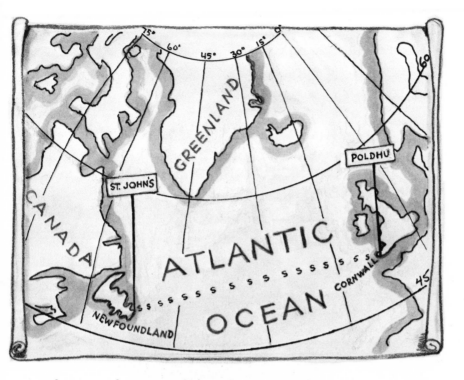

Academy and later had failed to pass the entrance examinations to the University of Bologna.

Bologna was Marconi's birthplace, but Guglielmo and his father both preferred Villa Grifone, their country estate outside the city. They had very different reasons. There, the boy, always at work on some mechanical gadget, could usually find the pieces he needed lying about. His father, who was a scholar, loved the peace and quiet of his country library, and took no interest whatever in his son's experiments.

Guglielmo's mother, who was Irish, did not especially like Villa Grifone. She preferred to spend her winters among the English residents of Leghorn or Florence. In 1887, when Guglielmo was thirteen, she enrolled him in The Leghorn Technical Institute, where he studied physics and electricity. When he failed to pass the entrance examinations to the University of Bologna, his mother persuaded one of the outstanding professors to let him set up experiments in his laboratory and also use the University Library. There Marconi read about Samuel Morse: how he came to invent the telegraph, how the Atlantic cable had been laid, connecting Europe and America. In Leghorn, he had already learned from an old telegraph operator how to tap out Morse code.

In 1894, when he was twenty, Marconi first heard of experiments by a German physicist named Hertz, who had died that year. In his obituary, Marconi read about experiments that Hertz had made with electromagnetic waves, and how they could be transmitted and received. Suddenly as he read, the idea of using these electromagnetic, or "Hertzian," waves for a wireless telegraph popped into his mind.

"The idea obsessed me," he said later. "I worked it all out in my imagination, but did not attempt experiments till back at Villa Grifone, in the autumn. Then two large rooms at the top of the house were set aside for me by my mother. There I began my experiments in earnest."

Nobody but he and his mother took his experiments seriously. Even his friend the professor thought it unlikely he would succeed, since scientists everywhere had been studying those electromagnetic, or radio, waves ever since Hertz had discovered them.

All winter he worked on his homemade apparatus of batteries, induction coils, and wires, which he based on descriptions published in scientific papers. So that he would not be disturbed, his mother carried up meals on a tray and left them outside the door. By early spring, she was invited to see what he had accomplished.

When he pressed a key down at one end of the attic, at the other end, thirty feet away, a buzzer sounded. Soon he was able to reach the main floor of the house, then the terrace, then a distance of over half a mile. A couple of his father's workmen helped him by carrying the receiver farther and farther away from his transmitter. By the end of the summer, he was sending waves and receiving signals from beyond a hill a mile away.

Whether the waves went OVER or THROUGH the hill, he did not know or care. The fact that they got there was all that concerned him.

This was as far as he could go by himself. Now he needed some financial backing to develop his wireless telegraph. Where could he get it?

His father, who so far had been paying for materials and equipment, learned that the family doctor knew the Italian ambassador in England. The doctor wrote the ambassador that Marconi wanted to offer his invention first to the Italian government. The ambassador found that the Italian government had no interest in it whatever. Therefore the young inventor and his mother left for England, arriving in London in February 1896.

The first demonstration Marconi made was on the roof of the General Post Office Building. The Chief Engineer thought that the wireless would be especially valuable in contacting ships and lighthouses and would reduce the loss of life from shipwrecks.

A year later, THE WIRELESS TELEGRAPH AND SIGNAL COMPANY LIMITED was formed, with more than one half of the 100,000 shares going to Marconi in return for the exclusive right to his now fully patented invention.

Marconi was away at the time. He was in Italy. After a visit with his father and mother, he went on to Rome. There, as a most distinguished Italian, he was presented to the king, Victor Emmanuel III, and his queen.

The next summer, back in England, he set up wireless communications between Queen Victoria, who was on the Isle of Wight, and her son Edward, the Prince of Wales, on the royal yacht in the bay, ten miles away.

In the spring of 1899, wireless stations had been built on both sides of the English Channel, connecting England and France. Now Marconi began to dream of sending messages across the Atlantic.

He travelled about inspecting the wireless stations being built all along the coast of England. In 1900 he acquired a new site at Poldhu, on the southwest coast of Cornwall. From there he was planning to send messages to America. For the American station, he chose a place as near as possible to Cornwall. This was Newfoundland.

It had been difficult for Marconi to persuade the company's board of directors to pay the cost of the overseas experiment. Many scientists said it would never work. They believed that since radio waves and light waves were both electromagnetic waves, and that since light waves travelled in straight lines, radio waves would do the same. They would either go shooting off into space or bury themselves in the ocean. They would never follow the curve of the earth. Marconi felt sure they would. He had already sent messages to ships below the horizon and they had been received. How the waves travelled, he did not know or care. The fact that they got there was all that concerned him.

At the end of November 1901, Marconi and two helpers sailed for St. John's, Newfoundland, to set up the receiving station. They carried kites and balloons to raise the aerial of the receiver as high as possible. Friday, December 6, they landed at St. John's. It was bitter cold. Monday they set up their equipment. Tuesday they sent a cablegram to Poldhu, saying that for three hours every afternoon the station should keep sending out by wireless the Morse code symbol for the letter *S*. Thursday, December 12, the weather was so stormy, the aerial broke. They launched another one. And that afternoon, not once, but three times Marconi was able to hear the three dots of the letter *S!*

He was prepared to have people say he had been mistaken, and was both surprised and delighted to have the *New York Times* report his attempt as "the most wonderful scientific development of modern times."

Victor Emmanuel III

NICHOLAS II

Marconi was back in England in time to see the King of Italy arrive on his royal yacht to attend the coronation ceremonies of King Edward VII. From there Marconi accompanied Victor Emmanuel III on a state visit to Tsar Nicholas II. They met at Kronstadt, the Russian naval base near St. Petersburg. The Tsar came aboard the Italian ship to see the wireless installation and hear the signals being transmitted and received.

The Italians saw "an air of goodness about the Tsar" and failed to understand why the Russian people saw him as a symbol of cruelty.

ЛЕНИН

ONE PERSON WHO COULD HAVE EXPLAINED
what was wrong with the Tsar and all that he stood for
was a young Russian, four years older than Marconi, who
in 1901 had just assumed the name of LENIN. This was
the man who was to destroy the old empire of the Tsars,
replace it with the world's first Communist nation, and
rule Russia until his death in 1924. Today his embalmed
body lies in a mausoleum in Moscow's Red Square, ven-
erated like the relics of a saint.

Brother

Mother

Father

Vladimir Ulyanov (11 years old)

Lenin's original name was Vladimir Ilyich Ulyanov. He was born in a city on the Volga, now called Ulyanovsk. His father, who was Superintendent of Education for the entire province, died in 1886, when Vladimir was sixteen.

The next year his older brother was executed for plotting to assassinate Tsar Alexander III, the father of the reigning Tsar, Nicholas II.

Greatly influenced by his brother's death, young Lenin continued to study his brother's books, especially the works of KARL MARX, the German philosopher, who had been exiled from his native land, and settled in England in 1849. Most thrilling to the boy was the COM-MUNIST MANIFESTO, in which Marx called upon the "workers of the world" to unite and overthrow the system under which they labored.

At first Lenin suffered from sharing his brother's last name. With the name of Ulyanov, he was put down by the police as a dangerous character. After a single term in law school, he was expelled from the University of Kazan. His mother then got permission for him to study at home and take his examination in St. Petersburg. He was so bright and worked so hard that he completed the four-year course in a single year. For a short time he practiced law in the small town of Samara, and then returned to St. Petersburg, where he soon joined a secret group of Marxists.

There one evening he met a big-eyed young teacher who was to become his wife. Nadezhda Krupskaya was her name. He called her Nadya. As they walked home together, Nadya told him that she taught a class in Communism to factory workers, and also how, disguised as a worker, she often went through the factories distributing Marxist leaflets.

During the fall of 1895, the Marxist group had been stirring up strike after strike in various factories. Lenin was among those arrested by the police and thrown into prison. He missed Nadya, but otherwise he did not mind being in prison too much—especially since books could be sent in and out. He and his friends sent secret messages hidden in the books' spine, and written in milk, which was invisible until the paper was heated.

After two years in prison, Lenin was sent as an exile to Siberia. The next year Nadya was sent to the same village, and they were married. In 1900, as soon as he could leave Siberia, Lenin bade farewell to his bride, and went at once to Switzerland to join a group of Russian Marxists living in Geneva.

There he started a journal to be smuggled in to the secret groups of Marxists living in Russia. He called it ISKRA, meaning "spark," for he hoped it would be a spark that would light the fires of revolution.

Next he wrote a book called WHAT IS TO BE DONE? in which he went far beyond the theories of Karl Marx. Marx believed that in every country business and industry would eventually grow so big and the owners so rich that the working class would finally rebel, seize control of the factories, and take over the government.

"This could never happen in Russia," declared Lenin. Russian workers and peasants could never carry out a revolution by themselves. They must be led by a party of revolutionists, dedicated to the destruction of privately owned business and the creation of a new society no longer divided between the too rich and the too poor.

"Give us an organization of revolutionists," Lenin declared, "and we will turn Russia upside down."

By 1903, Nadya had also left Siberia. She and Lenin were living in London. That summer forty Russian exiles met in London as delegates to the "All Russian Social Democratic Labor Party."

Lenin challenged the old party leader so violently with his radical ideas that he split the party in two. The majority who supported Lenin were called simply *Bolshevik* (meaning "majority").

These BOLSHEVIKS were to be the "organization of revolutionists" with which, in 1917, Lenin would "turn Russia upside down" as he had predicted.

HERE ARE MARIE AND PIERRE CURIE AT WORK
in 1902 in the cold, leaky shed in Paris where they discovered RADIUM. Though they had known it existed
since 1898, they saw it with their own eyes only after almost four years of hard work in the miserable shed.

Marie Curie's original name was Marya Sklodoska. She had been born in Poland, and had come to France to study chemistry at the University of Paris. There she met Pierre, who was a professor of physics. Soon after they were married, Marie began looking for an unexplored subject to use for her Doctor's degree in chemistry.

Just about this time, Henri Becquerel, a friend of the Curies, made a puzzling discovery. He had been trying to find out why certain substances continued to glow in the dark after having been exposed to sunlight. One day, to his surprise, he discovered in working with a rare metal called URANIUM that without having been exposed to the sun, it would spontaneously give off rays of light in the dark! Marie was filled with excitement at hearing about Henri Becquerel's mysterious rays.

Why should she not try to discover what caused these rays—this radiation, or RADIOACTIVITY as she soon suggested calling it? Having decided to do it, Marie could hardly wait to get started. First she must find a place to work. The Director of the University let her use an old storeroom, and there she started on what she called her "great adventure."

She began by measuring the electrical energy in the rays given off by uranium. To do this she used a very sensitive meter invented by Pierre and his brother. One day, examining the amount of uranium in a substance, she found the energy far greater than that given off by uranium alone. To make no mistake, she measured the rays again and again, with the same result.

"Some unknown element," she told Pierre, "must be causing those rays. It is surely there to be found."

Pierre, who had been keenly interested in Marie's work, now gave up his own study of crystals to join in the search for the unknown element.

By this time, they had a baby girl, Irene. During the day, she was under the watchful eye of her grandfather, Dr. Curie. But after a long hard day in the laboratory, Marie went home to wash and feed her baby.

Pierre and Marie, now working together, began their search with an ore called PITCHBLENDE, which contains uranium. First they took the ore apart chemically and tested each part for its radioactivity, throwing away the parts that were not radioactive, saving those that were. At last only two parts were left, one containing bismuth, the other barium (neither of which was radioactive by itself). This could only mean that there must be not one but TWO unknown elements to be found.

On June 6, 1898, Marie's laboratory notebook records great excitement, as both she and Pierre, working on separate experiments with the part containing bismuth, discovered the first of the two elements.

"What do you wish to name it?" asked Pierre.

"Could we call it POLONIUM?" said Marie, remembering her native Poland.

Then she went home to make gooseberry jelly and record the baby's weight in a special notebook, adding:

"Irene says thanks with her hand. She can walk very well now on all fours. She says 'gogli gogli go.' "

In July 1898 the Curies announced to the Academy of Science the existence of the new element, polonium.

In December 1898, they announced the existence of their second new element, which they called RADIUM, but which they had never actually seen.

Many scientists who read the second announcement were doubtful. To them seeing was believing.

"Show us your so-called radium," they demanded.

To do this, the Curies were faced with many problems. To begin with, they realized that what they were looking for was so tiny, they would need at least a hundred tons of pitchblende. Where could they get it? How could they pay for it? And where would they find a large enough workroom? The last question was answered first. Across the courtyard from the storeroom where they had been working was a large wooden shed with a skylight in the roof which leaked rain. It had no floor, a couple of old kitchen chairs, a discarded blackboard, and a rusty iron stove that gave little or no heat. The Director of the School of Physics, where Pierre was teaching, let them have the shed, and they moved in.

As for the pitchblende, they soon learned where it was to be found: in Bohemia, near a glass factory. The uranium (which they did not need) had been extracted for the making of glass, and the remaining dust thrown away in a nearby forest. This the Curies could have if they would pay to haul it to Paris. So they counted out their savings and sent them to Bohemia.

Marie was so excited when the first ton arrived she could not wait for the sacks to be carried into the shed.

Rushing out, she tore open a sack and sunk her hands deep in the brown dust. Now began four years of hard work which Marie said were "the best and happiest days of our lives. Sometimes I passed the whole day stirring a mass boiling in a great iron cauldron with an iron rod nearly as big as myself."

Time and again, huge wagons brought more and more tons of pitchblende to the courtyard gate. There stood Marie, her smoky overalls torn and spotted by acid, patiently stirring the last of the old lot or carrying in the result of her labors to Pierre who was working inside the shed.

At last came the day when she had her radium! Only one tenth of a gram of it came from a million times that amount of pitchblende. But there it was! She could see it and weigh it! The year was 1902.

One evening Marie and Pierre were sitting at home. Irene, now four years old, was asleep. Marie was making an apron for her. Suddenly she put down her sewing and proposed going back to the shed to see the radium again.

"Don't light the lamp," she said when they got there, pointing to a small dish. There shining in the dark was their precious radium—less than half a teaspoonful—giving off enough light to read by.

In December 1903, Marie and Pierre Curie shared the Nobel Prize for Science with Henri Becquerel for their joint discovery.

PART 2

1903
TO
1905

GLIDER

IN SEPTEMBER 1903, THE WRIGHT BROTHERS took their new flying machine in sections to Kitty Hawk. It was a glider of the same design as their previous one, with a four-cylinder, twelve-horsepower gasoline engine.

By the time they had the two parts assembled, stormy

+ ENGINE

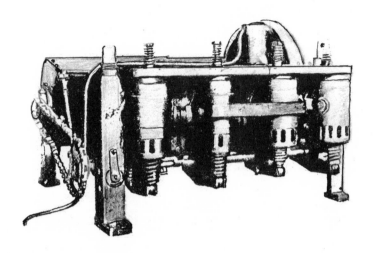

= *FLYING MACHINE*

weather set in. Next they discovered that a propeller shaft had cracked. Orville had to return to Dayton for another one, and did not get back to Kitty Hawk until Friday, December 11.

Saturday the plane was repaired, but the wind was too light. On Sunday and Monday there was still not enough wind to start from level ground, so they decided to take off from the top of Kill Devil Hill.

They had invited several people to see their flight, and put up a signal when they were ready to start. Soon four men appeared and helped roll the machine in place.

The Wrights then tossed a coin to see who should be the pilot. Wilbur won, climbed aboard, lay face down on the lower plane. Orville stood at one of the wings to help balance the machine as it took off, but it started off so fast that, as he said later:

"I could stay with it only a few feet. It climbed a few feet, stalled and then settled to the ground near the foot of the hill. The left wing touched first and several parts were broken. . . . It took two days to make the repairs. . . . During the night a strong wind blew in from the north. By ten the next morning [December 17] although the wind was as strong as ever we decided to try another flight, and hung out the signal.

"The biting cold made it difficult to work, [but] by the time all was ready, three members of the Life Saving Station and two other men were there.

"Wilbur had used his turn, so the first trial belonged to me. Wilbur ran at the side of the machine, holding the wing in balance. Facing a twenty-seven-mile wind, it started so slowly, Wilbur was able to stay with it until it lifted into the air."

Orville's flight lasted twelve seconds; he flew one hundred and twenty feet. The brothers made three more flights. Wilbur's was the longest—fifty-nine seconds. This was the last one, because, said Orville:

"While we were standing about discussing this last flight, a sudden gust of wind struck the machine and began to turn it over and over. Everybody made a rush for it . . . in vain. The ribs of the machine were broken, the motor injured, so that all possibility of further flights for that year were at an end."

The machine, what was left of it, was put away in the shed. The brothers and their friends had lunch in their hut, washed the dishes, and then set off over the windy sand dunes for the Kitty Hawk Weather Station where they sent this telegram to their father in Dayton:

SUCCESS. FOUR FLIGHTS THURSDAY MORNING. ALL AGAINST TWENTY-SEVEN MILE WIND. STARTED FROM LEVEL WITH ENGINE POWER ALONE. AVERAGE SPEED THROUGH AIR TWENTY-ONE MILES. LONGEST 59 SECONDS. INFORM PRESS. HOME CHRISTMAS.

ORVILLE WRIGHT.

This was the modest announcement of a great event that was to mark a turning point in man's life on earth. But the next morning only three newspapers in the entire United States reported it. And not one of the three put this news on the front page.

When they telegraphed their father the good news, the telegraph operator in Norfolk, Virginia, wanted to know if it would be all right to give the news to a reporter friend of his.

The brothers said no. They wanted to let the Dayton newspaper make the original announcement. But the Dayton newspaper did not think the news was worth mentioning!

Cartoon from the N.Y. Herald

THE WINTER OF 1903, THEODORE ROOSEVELT was "dee-lighted" to be signing a treaty that would insure the digging of the Panama Canal! To connect the Atlantic and Pacific Oceans at the Isthmus of Panama was not a new idea. The French had tried to build a canal there and failed.

The United States had long wanted to. They had built a railroad in Panama, but could make no agreement about a canal, because Colombia (to which Panama belonged) was having one revolution after another, with power being seized by a new set of greedier bandits.

"You could no more make an agreement with the rulers of Colombia," declared Theodore Roosevelt, "than you could nail currant jelly to the wall."

So he gave up trying and used a more direct method, when he heard that another revolution was going on in Colombia—the 54th one in 53 years!

Panama was fighting for independence. So Roosevelt sent U.S. Marines there to prevent Colombian soldiers from going into Panama on the railroad which had been built by the United States. Thus protected, little Panama gained her independence.

One morning in November 1903, word reached the White House that the Republic of Panama had been proclaimed. One week later, a treaty with the new Republic had been signed and the United States had purchased the Canal Zone for $40,000,000. At last! What had needed to be done for many years had been speedily accomplished.

Colombia was furious. And there were those in the United States who were critical of what had been done, but Roosevelt felt he had done no wrong.

"If I had waited for Congress," said he, "they would have debated for another fifty years. I took the Isthmus, started the Canal, and left the Congress not to debate the Canal, but to debate me."

In November 1906, Theodore Roosevelt became the first President ever to leave the United States while he was in office. He was on his way to Panama to see how the great work he had set in motion was coming along.

In a letter to his son Kermit, he describes three interesting days he spent where the digging had begun:

"I went over the ground of the Gatun and La Boca dams . . . and spent a day in the Culebra cut where the great work is being done. There huge steam shovels are hard at it; scooping [up] huge masses of rock and gravel and dirt, previously loosened by the drillers and dynamite blasters, loading it onto trains which take it away to some dump either in the jungle or where the dams are to be built. They are eating steadily into the mountain, cutting it down and down. . . .

"The Gatun dam will make a lake miles long and the railroad now goes at what will be the bottom of this lake . . . it was curious to think that in a few years great ships would be floating in water a hundred feet above where we were. . . ."

It would be 1914 before the Panama Canal was completed and the first ship sailed through.

HENRY FORD BUILT HIS FIRST AUTOMOBILE IN
1896. That was the year that the Wright brothers decided it would be easier to build a flying machine.

In 1903, when the Wrights made their successful
flight at Kitty Hawk, Henry Ford and eleven other
stockholders founded the Ford Motor Company.

At first, like Olds, Duryea, and all the other early manufacturers, the Ford Motor Company made automobiles that only the very rich could afford to buy. But it was not long before Ford himself came to believe that no matter what a man's income was, he should be able to own an automobile.

Ford's idea of making cheap cars did not appeal to the other stockholders. They began to argue with him. Ford could not stand an argument, so he bought 58 percent of the stock and did as he pleased.

This meant a complete change in the way cars were being made. Instead of having each car put together individually, Ford worked out a system called an assembly line by which the parts of many cars could be sent along to the workers on conveyor belts.

This saved so much time and money that by 1908 he was able to bring out his first MODEL T at a price of $980. He now set the goal of "a car a minute," and each

1 9 0 8

THE MODEL T

year he planned to reduce the price of the Model T.

By 1913 he was able to sell the Model T, or the "Tin Lizzy" as it was then being called, for $500.

By 1918 a thousand cars a day were coming off the assembly line and the Ford Motor Company had become the largest producer of automobiles in the world.

The next year, Henry Ford bought all of the stock and so became the sole owner of that giant company.

THIS CARTOON SHOWS PRESIDENT ROOSEVELT
standing between the Tsar of Russia and the Emperor of
Japan, arranging a treaty for which he was to be awarded
the Nobel Prize for Peace. Actually the treaty was signed
by two delegates from each of the two nations meeting
with the President in Portsmouth, New Hampshire.

This peace treaty, which was signed in 1905, ended
the Russo-Japanese War, which had been started by tiny

Japan against gigantic Russia, the largest country in the world.

For a number of years, the Japanese had been alarmed to see the Russians edging farther and farther eastward into Manchuria and becoming more and more involved in the affairs of Korea. And when Russia leased from China the Liaotung Peninsula and built a naval base at Port Arthur, that was too much for Japan to endure.

On February 8, 1904, without warning, the Japanese fleet attacked the Russian fleet at Port Arthur and the war was on! Russia seemed so much more powerful than Japan that people all over the world expected Japan to be defeated. The world was in for a surprise.

First the Japanese warships bottled up what was left of the Russian fleet in Port Arthur, and after a siege of two months the port surrendered. On land the Japanese army drove the Russians back through Manchuria, after defeating them at the battle of Mukden. A Russian fleet that had come all the way from the Baltic Sea was smashed by the Japanese in the straits of Tsushima.

By that time both countries wanted the war to end. Russia's government was in trouble at home. To begin with, the eastern expansion was considered useless by most Russian people, so the resulting war was unpopular. And Russia's rapid defeat helped to bring on the Russian Revolution of 1905.

RUSSIA'S
DOUBLE EAGLE

1905

IT WAS LESS THAN THREE YEARS AFTER THE miners' strike in Pennsylvania had been settled peaceably and the new Department of Labor added to the United States government, when in Russia, strikes in mines and factories turned into an actual revolution.

It began with "Bloody Sunday." On Sunday, January 22, a procession of workers, led by Father Gapon, a Russian Orthodox priest, appeared before the Winter Palace in St. Petersburg, carrying icons and crosses, but no guns or weapons of any kind. They were on strike and had come to beg the Tsar for better working conditions.

But the Tsar was not there, and the troops guarding the palace fired on the unarmed workingmen, killing seventy of them and wounding two hundred and forty.

Spring and summer were filled with strikes in mines and factories, outbreaks among the peasants, and even mutiny in the army and navy. Following a citywide strike in St. Petersburg, various trades organized the first SOVIET, or council of workers.

By the end of October, the Tsar felt obliged to promise certain reforms in the government. He granted some voting rights and established a DUMA, or Parliament. He also pardoned all political exiles, Lenin included.

In November, Lenin was back in Russia, calling for a massive revolt. Strikes broke out in Moscow, followed by strikes in other cities. Soon these strikes turned into actual revolution! By the end of December, the revolution had been stamped out. But even so, Lenin considered it a valuable experience. For the first time Russian workingmen had fought against the army of the Tsar. Years later he declared:

"Without the general rehearsal of 1905, the victorious Revolution of 1917 would not have been possible."

西
太
后

TODAY CHINA, LIKE RUSSIA, IS A COMMUNIST
nation, but in 1905, China, too, was an empire—the
oldest empire in the world. This is the Dowager Empress, TZU HSI, the last powerful ruler of the Manchu

Dynasty, a strong-willed, hot-tempered woman of seventy, known as the "old Buddha."

This is SUN YAT-SEN, thirty-one years younger than the Empress. In 1911 he started a revolution against the Manchu Dynasty. In 1912 he founded the Republic of China and became its first President.

The boy is MAO TSE-TUNG, recent leader of Communist China. He was just seven years old in 1900, when the great change began with the Boxer Rebellion.

The Boxer Rebellion was an attempt to cure the ills of China by driving out all "foreign devils." Bands of armed men who called themselves "Fists of Righteousness" (nicknamed Boxers) roamed the countryside, murdering foreign missionaries, tearing up railroad tracks, ripping out telephone wires, destroying all the inventions the hated foreigners had brought with them to China.

The Empress, going against the advice of her wisest ministers, supported the Boxers and ordered a massacre of all foreigners, an order seized upon by the Boxers. They besieged the foreign embassies in Peking, and even murdered the German ambassador in the street.

It was not long before troops from the Western nations were in China. And when the peace terms were dictated, the Empress was obliged to pay such a huge amount of money as to keep China poor for years to come.

Sun Yat-sen was not in China during the Boxer Rebellion. He was in Japan, having just returned from a tour of Europe and the United States aimed at gaining support for his revolution against the Manchu Dynasty.

Little Mao Tse-tung could not have heard much, if anything, about the Boxer Rebellion, since it took place mostly in northern China. And he lived in the southern province of Hunan, in a tiny village at least 900 miles from Peking. His birthplace was the typical peasant's house, thatched with rice straw, red peppers hanging from the roof beams, and a pigsty attached to one end.

Mao grew up loving his gentle mother. But he hated and feared his violent father, who kept his wife and sons in order by beating them. Mao was only five when he was put to work in the rice paddies, or weeding beans, watering buffalo, or gathering wood for charcoal. At seven, he spent part of each day learning to read and write, which was far more to his liking.

In 1911, he was in the Tungshan Higher Primary School when one of Sun Yat-sen's officers spoke to his class. Five days later Mao and a friend left to join the Revolutionary army. Within months the Manchu Empire had collapsed and the new Republic had taken its place.

The next year of real importance in Mao's life was 1918. He was in Peking, working in the University Library. There he first read the *Communist Manifesto* by Karl Marx, which had just been translated into Chinese.

PART 3

1905
TO
1909

ORVILLE (1908) WILBUR

AT FIRST, THE WRIGHT BROTHERS HAD not been greatly disturbed by the lack of interest in their invention. They were too busy thinking up new ways to improve their machine, now that the actual problem of flying had been solved. As soon as they got back from Kitty Hawk, they began building what they called the WRIGHT FLYER II.

Turning over to their chief mechanic the work in the bicycle shop, they spent their time flying the new plane from a cow pasture about eight miles from Dayton.

By spring they felt ready to invite a number of Dayton newspapermen to watch them fly their new improved machine. But that day the engine stalled; they could not even get the plane off the ground. And the press left laughing at the whole ridiculous idea of flying!

Even their enthusiastic friend and supporter, Octave Chanute, did not fully foresee the future of the "flying machine." In an article for the March issue of the *Popular Science Monthly,* he wrote:

"Its first use will probably be military. . . . It may even carry mail . . . but the loads will be very small. . . . The machines will be used in sport . . . but never as commercial carriers."

The Wrights also believed that the first use of the airplane would be military, and wanted to offer it first to their own government. Therefore in January 1905 they offered their invention to the United States War Department. And the War Department flatly rejected the offer.

However, the next month, the Wrights received a letter from the British War Department, and later that year another from the Aero Club of France, as well as from the French War Department.

"Ah well," said Wilbur to Orville, "we took pains to see that Opportunity gave a good clear knock on our own War Department door."

Again they went back to work and spent another year developing and improving their engine. In the spring of 1907 Wilbur went to England. After a brief unsatisfactory visit, he cabled Orville to join him in Paris.

The airplane was crated and sent by rail to New York, and shipped from there to France. Nothing came of the negotiations with the French War Department, so the brothers returned home leaving the plane behind, still in its crate.

And then to their amazement, they heard from the United States War Department!

How had this come about? Through the Secretary of War, William Howard Taft.

Who had asked him to see about this? Who else but that energetic, enterprising man, Theodore Roosevelt.

"I'd like to have you look into the claims of those Wright brothers," Roosevelt said to Taft one morning.

"I hear they have been trying in vain to get the army to listen to their claims."

So at last, over four years after they had made their historic flight, the Wright brothers were called in by the War Department.

"We can build an airplane," they said "that will fly long enough and fast enough to be used by the army."

"Prove it," demanded the War Department.

To do this, the Wrights said they would need $25,000 to cover their expenses. The army was at a loss to know how or where to get this amount of money.

Finally three courageous young army officers made up their minds to go directly to the White House and consult the person most likely to come up with an idea.

"Twenty-five thousand dollars!" exclaimed T. R. in a gruff voice. "That's a lot of money!"

He sat for a moment. Then he slapped his hand on his desk, jumped to his feet, rushed to a filing cabinet, and took out a thin yellow folder.

"Gentlemen," he grinned, "I've got it! An even twenty-five thousand dollars!"

His marvelous memory had served him well. Ten years earlier, during the Spanish-American War, he explained, Congress had set aside that amount of money to be used by the President how and when it was needed. It had never been used. There was no time limit. All that was lacking was his signature. Here it is:

Theodore Roosevelt

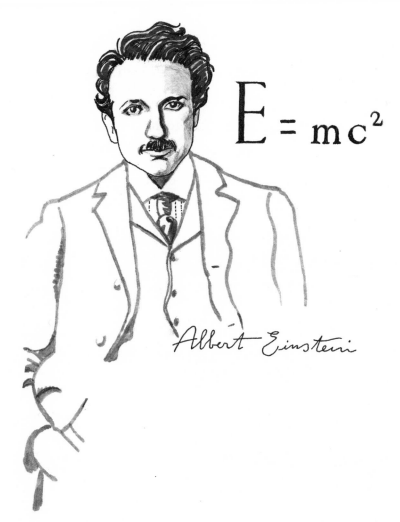

$$E = mc^2$$

Albert Einstein

THIS IS THE FAMOUS EQUATION THAT
solved a mystery and this is Albert Einstein, the very
brilliant young scientist who in 1905 made the discovery
that lies behind it.

73

The mystery was one that had baffled scientists ever since Becquerel discovered that uranium was radioactive and the Curies had gone on to discover two more minerals able to give off light and heat, in huge quantities over long periods of time. This was puzzling to scientists since it was so different from the way other things give off energy by *burning,* like coal or gas or wood.

This was Einstein's answer: $E = mc^2$.

E stands for ENERGY.

m stands for MASS, or MATTER.

c^2 is a *huge* number. If c, the speed of light, is measured in centimeters per second, c^2 is 900,000,000,000,000,000,000.

The equal sign means ENERGY and MATTER are the same thing. Matter is simply a much more highly concentrated form of energy. A tiny amount of matter, like radium, can be *transformed* into an enormous amount of energy.

This was almost impossible for scientists in general to accept. It was too revolutionary. It upset everything they had been taught to believe about matter and energy. Einstein also upset their old beliefs about TIME, SPACE, and MOTION with his

Albert
(6 years old)
with
his sister

THEORY OF RELATIVITY

a paper which he published in 1905 and which led to his famous equation, $E = mc^2$.

Now, since an ATOM was the smallest known division of matter and matter was concentrated energy, this equation gave a reason for trying to split the atom and release its energy—its ATOMIC ENERGY. This was not to happen until 1942. By that time Albert Einstein was world-famous and had become a citizen of the United States.

Einstein had been born in 1879 in the German city of Ulm. As he did not begin to talk until he was three, his

worried parents were beginning to think that their dear little Albert must be not very bright.

By then the family had moved to Munich, where his father and his Uncle Jacob, who lived with the family, started a small electrochemical factory.

Albert was only four or five when he first became excited by the magical world of science. One day when he was in bed recovering from some slight illness, his father came home with a present for him.

It was a compass—a mariner's compass. The little boy took it in his hands. He turned it around and around. But no matter which way he turned it, the arrow kept pointing in the same direction. What could possibly be in there that he could not see?

When he was nine or ten, his introduction to mathematics came from his Uncle Jacob.

"What is algebra?" Albert asked his uncle.

"Algebra," said his uncle, "is a puzzle in arithmetic. When you don't know something you call it X and then you try to find it."

Albert loved puzzles. So he loved to solve algebra problems, but in his own way—not by any set of rules!

In school he objected to learning anything word for word. Languages bored him. But he was so far ahead in mathematics that he often embarrassed his teachers by asking them questions they were unable to answer.

He was in the gymnasium, or junior high school, when his father's business failed and the family moved to Milan, Italy. All except Albert.

He applied to the Swiss Federal Polytechnic School in Zurich, Switzerland, but failed to pass the entrance examinations. He was too weak in languages.

However, his skill in mathematics was so amazing that the Director arranged for him to complete the entrance requirements in another Swiss school, and in less than a year Albert entered the Polytechnic School.

He had not been there long before he made up his mind to become a teacher of physics. He had also met and fallen in love with a girl from Hungary, Mileva Maritsch. Long before graduation, they were planning to marry as soon as Albert was able to become a teacher.

In 1900, he graduated and began looking for a teach-, ing position, but in spite of his great ability, no one would hire him. He could not get a job. He was hungry and practically in rags, when a former classmate saw him and introduced him to the Director of the government Patent Office in the capital city of Bern.

In 1902, he started his new job as an examiner in the Patent Office. It was easy work and gave him plenty of time to spend on the very special paper on physics and mathematics he was writing.

In 1903, he and Mileva were married.

In 1904, the first of their two sons was born.

And the next year was that all-important one of 1905, when the paper which he had been writing in his time off from the Patent Office was published. And for the first time the world became aware of the famous equation which was to unlock the door to the ATOMIC AGE, in which we are now living.

DR. SIGMUND FREUD, THE FOUNDER OF PSY-
choanalysis, was another person who was to cause a great
revolution in thinking. His life's work was based on the
fact that the unconscious mind greatly influences a
person's actions—an idea that was not to be generally
accepted for many years.

This was not in the least surprising to Dr. Freud.

In 1900, he had been the author of a book called THE INTERPRETATION OF DREAMS, which had been practically ignored. In a letter to a friend, Freud wrote that his "dream child" had been a "respectable flop" and went on to say that the theories that he and his friend held were "so far ahead of our time that we should expect no recognition of them in our lifetime."

Freud was then forty-four years old. He had a wife, Martha, and a large, happy family of six children ranging in age from thirteen to five, who were his "great pride."

In 1902, he was made Professor of Nervous Diseases at the University of Vienna. And what did he teach?

First, that the unconscious mind was a storehouse of memories; that these memories could cause nervous and mental illness. And that such illness could often be cured by bringing these memories into the conscious mind. The best way for a person to do this was to try to remember his dreams and have them interpreted.

"When one is asleep," said Freud, "those memories stored away in the unconscious mind come to the surface in the form of dreams."

In addition to analyzing thousands of patients' dreams before writing his now-famous *The Interpretation of Dreams,* he studied his own dreams, which led to memories of his childhood.

Getting these memories out in the open did much to relieve the nervous headaches, fears, and periods of depression from which he had always suffered.

One dream he had had was of a one-eyed man whom he seemed to fear and dislike. The only one-eyed man he could recall was a schoolteacher whom he had liked very much. When he asked his mother who the one-eyed man he had dreamed about could possibly be, she said, "That must be the doctor who sewed up your cheek after you fell off a stool and cut it open. You were about three years old."

Freud did not remember the accident at all. But his fear and resentment toward the doctor had been festering in his unconscious memory.

Even as a grown man Freud had always had a strange fear of riding on trains, until he dreamed of a terrifying train trip he had taken as a child. Then, by knowing the reason for his fear, he was able to overcome it.

It was about 1904 when Dr. Freud first heard from a much younger Swiss psychologist by the name of

CARL GUSTAV JUNG

Jung had been drawn to Freud's theories after reading *The Interpretation of Dreams*. Dr. Jung, a professor at the Psychiatric Clinic in Zurich, paid his first visit to Dr. Freud in February 1907.

"We met at one o'clock in the afternoon," Jung said, "and talked virtually without pause for thirteen hours. Freud was the first man of real importance I had met. I found him altogether remarkable!"

And Freud found Jung bright and thoroughly charming and soon began to think of him as a favorite son.

In December 1908, Freud received a letter from the President of Clark University in Worcester, Massachusetts, inviting him to give a course of lectures there the following August. In June he was glad to hear that Jung had also been invited to lecture at Clark University. They arranged to meet at the German seaport of Bremen. From there they embarked on the six-day voyage to America. Every day they spent the otherwise idle hours analyzing each other's dreams.

The lectures Freud gave were delivered in German. At the end of the series, Clark University conferred an honorary degree on Dr. Sigmund Freud. His voice broke slightly as he accepted the honor, saying:

"This is the first official recognition of my work." And yet that recognition—contrary to his earlier prediction—had come well within his lifetime.

He remained at the University of Vienna until 1938, when Austria was occupied by Nazi Germany and the cry of "Heil Hitler" was heard in the streets.

As a Jew, Freud was no longer safe in Vienna. He escaped to London, where he died the following year at the age of eighty-three.

90° NORTH

90° NORTH

THE YEAR 1908 WAS WHEN ROBERT PEARY SET
out on what he knew would be his last trip to the Arctic.
He was fifty-two years old. For twenty years he had been
trying to reach the North Pole.

In 1905, his fifth voyage had been made in his new
ship, the ROOSEVELT, named for the President. In
1908, the *Roosevelt,* on its way north again, left New
York harbor on July 8, and sailed to the northernmost
shore of Greenland. Peary planned to spend the winter in
Greenland, in order to start across the ocean of ice well
before the polar cap began to thaw and crack.

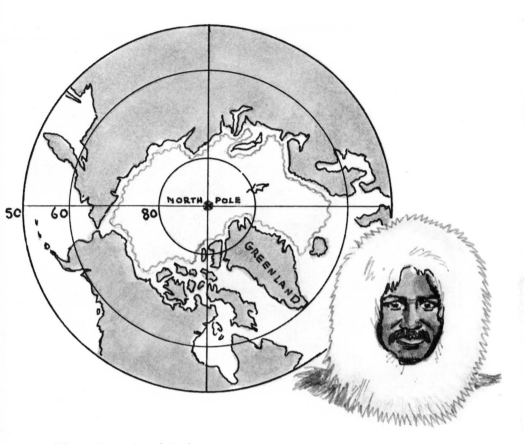

The Greenland Eskimos were always glad to see their
good friend Peary return. As one of them said:

"You are like the sun, Peary-asoah. You always come
back. I think, when the Almighty Devil takes your body
away, your Spirit will still come to us."

Another explorer friend always welcomed back by the
Eskimos was Matthew Henson, a black man who had been
Peary's right-hand man on every previous expedition.

On March 1, 1909, the explorers left Greenland behind and began their actual journey toward the Pole.
From now on they would be walking directly over the
frozen sea, crossing fields of ice, which continually
creaked and groaned and often cracked open into chan-
nels or "leads" of dark green water.

The expedition started out with nineteen sledges, one

hundred thirty-three dogs, seventeen Eskimos, five white men, and the black man Matthew Henson, who, Peary declared, was almost as skillful as an Eskimo in handling the dogs and sledges. For food they carried hardtack, tea, condensed milk, and a form of dried meat called PEM-MICAN, lightweight and very satisfying.

They had travelled north exactly one month and were just short of 88 degrees latitude, when on April 1, most of the party turned back, leaving Peary, Henson, and four Eskimos—Ootah, Ooqueah, Eginwah, and Seeglo—to make the last lap of the journey. They had five sledges and the forty best dogs. There were 133 miles left to go.

Peary planned to cover the distance in five marches, which should bring them to the Pole by noon of the fifth day. This is from Peary's own record of the last five days:

APRIL 2: A little after midnight, after a few hours of sound, warm refreshing sleep [inside the igloo] and a hearty breakfast, I started [on] the trail north. It was a fine marching morning, clear and sunlit, with a temperature of minus 25. We travelled 10 hours without stopping, covering 30 miles. While we were building our igloos, we could see to the east a wide lead opening up. The approaching full moon was evidently getting in its work [on the tides]. As we travelled on, the moon circled round and round the heavens opposite the sun, a disc of silver opposite a disc of gold.

APRIL 3: We woke early after a few hours sleep. As daylight is now continuous, we could travel as long as we pleased and sleep as long as we must. We hustled along for 10 hours again, but making only 20 miles because of a brief delay at a narrow lead. All day long, we heard the ice grinding and groaning on all sides. Each day when we stopped to make camp, the Eskimos would climb some pinnacle of ice and strain their eyes to the north wondering if the "pole" was yet in sight.

Again we travelled for 10 hours straight and reeled off at APRIL 4: least 25 miles. Near the end of the day we crossed a lead about 100 miles wide on young ice so thin that as I ran ahead to guide the dogs, I was obliged to slide my feet and travel wide, bear style, to distribute my weight. The last two men came over on all fours. As one of the sledges neared the north side, a runner cut clear through the ice, and I expected every moment that the whole thing, dogs and all, would go through the ice and down to the bottom. But it did not. The temperature was then minus 35. The bitter wind burned our faces so that they cracked and pained so that we could hardly go to sleep.

At our camp, I gave the party a little more sleep, as we APRIL 5: were all pretty well played out. I took a latitude sight and this indicated our position to be 80 degrees and 25 minutes, or 35 miles from the Pole. Before midnight we were on the trail again. When we had covered a good 15 miles, we halted, made tea, ate lunch and rested the dogs. In 12 hours actual travelling time we had made 30 miles.

The last march northward ended at 10 o'clock in the APRIL 6: forenoon. I made the first observation at our polar camp.

It indicated our position as 89 degrees and 57 minutes. We were now at the end of our upward journey. The Pole at last! My dream and goal of twenty years! I cannot bring myself to realize it. . . . After I had planted the American flag in the ice, I told Henson to time the Eskimos in three rousing cheers which they gave with greatest enthusiasm. . . . Then in a space between the ice blocks, I deposited a glass bottle containing a strip of my flag and the following record.

90 N. Lat., North Pole.

April 6, 1909

I have today hoisted the national ensign of the United States of America at this place, which my observations indicate to be the North Polar axis of the earth and have formally taken possession of the entire region in the name of the President of the United States. I leave this record and the United States flag in possession.

Robert E. Peary
United States Navy

FOR THE WRIGHT BROTHERS THE YEAR 1908
was filled with success. In February, their bid was accepted by the War Department. In March, they sold the
right to build their planes in France for $100,000. In
April, they went to Kitty Hawk to practice for demon-
strations to be made later that summer in both North

America and France. The plane they took with them differed from the others they had made.

They no longer had to ride lying face down. They had rearranged the control levers for use in a sitting position, and there was a seat for a passenger.

It was decided that Orville should make the tests for the War Department, while Wilbur went to France. The French people still did not believe that this man from America could fly. He took off from a racecourse about ninety miles southwest of Paris, and when he went soaring over their heads like a bird, the crowd went wild. He stayed in France until the end of the year, pleasing everyone by his modesty, his good humor, and his willingness to share his knowledge so long as he did not have to make a formal speech.

"I know only one bird, the parrot, that can speak," he explained "and it can't fly very high."

Orville, meanwhile, was having great success at Fort Meyer, Virginia, near Washington, D.C., with his tests for the War Department. The officers were amazed, the spectators wildly excited, as he banked round and round the parade ground, continually breaking his own records.

On September 9, he circled the field 57 times in 57 minutes and 35 seconds. He invited one of the young officers who had gone to the White House and received the $25,000 from the President to go for a ride.

On the last day of the tests, there was a tragedy. Orville had as his passenger another young officer. The propeller cracked. The plane crashed. Orville was injured. The young officer was killed.

July 30, 1909, the United States War Department received its first military plane and paid the Wright brothers $30,000 for it. At long last, even the most skeptical were convinced that flying was a reality.

Robert Peary, who had just returned from the North Pole, spoke with great enthusiasm about aviation.

"There is a new art in the world today," he said, "the art of flying. A new world to conquer, the world of the atmosphere. A new ocean to navigate, the ocean of air whose only coasts are infinite space."

INDEX

Swiss Federal Polytechnic School, 77
Swiss Patent Office, 78

Taft, William Howard, 70
"Teddy Bear" (toy), 23
Theory of relativity, 74–75
Tungshan Higher Primary School, 66
Tzu Hsi, Dowager Empress, 63–64

Ulyanov, Vladimir Ilyich, *see* Lenin, Nikolai
U.S. Constitution, 20, 23
U.S. Department of Commerce, 22
U.S. Department of Labor, 22, 61
U.S. War Department, 69, 70, 72, 91, 92, 93
University of Bologna, 25, 26–27
University of Kazan, 35

University of Paris, 39
University of Vienna, 80, 83
Uranium, 39, 42

Victor Emmanuel III, King, 29, 32
Victoria, Queen, 6, 30

Weather Bureau (Washington, D.C.), 17
What Is to Be Done? (Lenin), 36–37
Wireless Telegraph and Signal Company Limited, 29
Wright, Bishop, 14
Wright, Wilbur and Orville, 13–19, 55, 68–72, 91–93; childhood interests of, 14–15; flying machine experiments, 16–19; Kitty Hawk flight (1903), 46–50
Wright Flyer II, 68